A PASSION FOR

Horses

PHOTOGRAPHY BY CHRISTIANE SLAWIK

Published by Willow Creek Press, Inc.
P.O. Box 147, Minocqua, Wisconsin 54548

Design: Donnie Rubo
Printed in China

A PASSION FOR

Horses

PHOTOGRAPHY BY CHRISTIANE SLAWIK

✚ WILLOW CREEK PRESS®

Passion

The object of an intense desire, ardent
affection, or enthusiasm.

—*World English Dictionary*

Christiane Slawik's incomparable images capture
the grace, strength, courage and kindness of horses.
Her passion for these magnificent animals is on full
and dynamic display in this unique volume that
fuses her award-winning photography with
classic horse passages.

is always beautiful.

—*Walt Whitman*

The

wind

of heaven is that which blows

between a horse's ears.

—*Arabian proverb*

Every horse is a

mystery.

—Bill Barich

You know I love to spend
my morning time, like sunlight

dancing

on your skin.

—Rodney Crowell

The
eternal
and wonderful sight of horses
at liberty is magical to watch.

—*Bertrand Leclair*

Horses leave hoofprints on your

heart.

—*Unknown*

A horse in the

wind,

a perfect symphony.

—*Unknown*

He

soared

over every fence as if he had wings.

—Stephen Budiansky

His

hooves

pound the beat,

your heart

sings the song.

—*Jerry Shulman*

For one to fly, one needs only to take the

reins.

—*Melissa James*

Honor

lies in the mane of a horse.

—*Herman Melville*

Riding

is one of those pastimes which once
experienced is never forgotten.

—Jane Holderness-Roddam

Fierce

as the fire and fleet as the wind...

—A. L. Gordon

Horses make a landscape look more

beautiful.

—*Alice Walker*

Horses

lend us the wings we lack.

—*Pam Brown*

Only when you see
through the

eyes

of the horse, can you lead
the dance of the mind.

—*Pete Spates*

There are many wonderful
places in the

world,

but one of my favorite places
is on the back of my horse.

—*Unknown*

O, for a horse with

wings!

—William Shakespeare

Of all creatures, the horse is the

noblest.

—*Gervase Markham*

Rarely do great beauty and great

virtue

dwell together.

—*Francesco Petrarca*

Nothing is so strong as

gentleness,

nothing so gentle as real strength.

—*Saint Francis de Sales*

A lovely horse is always an

experience...

It is an emotional experience of the
kind that is spoiled by words.

—*Beryl Markham*

There is no

secret

so close as that between

a rider and his horse.

—*Robert Smith Surtees*

Look closely. The beautiful may be

small.

—Immanuel Kant

A horse is a thing of such beauty…
none will tire of looking at him as
long as he displays himself in his

splendor.

—Xenophon

A horse is a beautiful animal, but it is
perhaps most remarkable because it

moves

as if it always hears music.

—*Mark Helprin*

The delicate and exquisite

horse is itself a work of

art.

—*Bertrand Leclair*

Let a horse whisper in your ear and

breathe

on your heart. You will never regret it.

—*Unknown*

They are more beautiful than anything
in the world, kinetic sculptures,
perfect form in

motion.

—Kate Millett

By reason of his

elegance,

he resembles an image painted in a palace,

though he is as majestic as the palace itself.

—*Abd al-Qadir*

To

ride

a horse is to ride the sky.

—*Unknown*

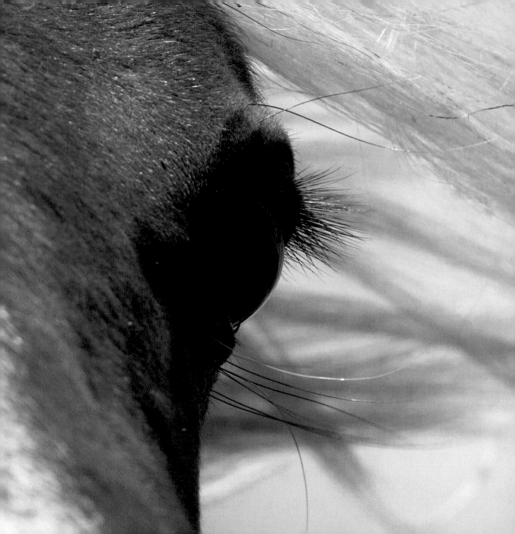

Your eyes show the strength of your

soul.

—*Paulo Coelho*

If you have seen nothing but the beauty
of their markings and limbs, their true

beauty

is hidden from you.

—*Al Mutanabbi*

Ask me to show you

in motion and I will

show you a horse.

—*Unknown*

In riding a horse we borrow

freedom.

—Helen Thomson

Over the centuries the
horse and his movement
have been an

inspiration

to artists, poets,
and writers.

—*Susan E. Harris*

God forbid that I should go to any

Heaven

in which there are no horses.

—*R.B. Cunninghame-Graham*

When riding a horse we leave our fear, troubles, and sadness behind on the *ground.*

—Judi Carlson

The best

mirror

is an old friend.

—*George Herbert*

The world is best

viewed

through the ears
of a horse.

—*Unknown*

The essential joy of being with
horses is that it brings us in contact
with the rare elements of

grace,

beauty, spirit,
and fire.

—*Sharon Ralls Lemon*

Dance

above ground, never descending. Grace
incarnate. Passion on hooves.

—*Unknown*

He

trots

the air; the earth sings when he touches
it; the basest horn of his hoof is more
musical than the pipe of Hermes.

—William Shakespeare

The

outside

of a horse is good for

the inside of a man.

—*Sir Winston Churchill*

To many, the words love, hope, and dreams are synonymous with

horses.

—*Oliver Wendell Holmes, Sr.*